WHAT MAKES AMERICA GREAT

Bob Dowell

Ordering Information:

For orders and inquiries, please contact:
1-888-375-9818
www.toplinkpublishing.com
bookorder@toplinkpublishing.com

Printed in the United States of America

DEAR READER

This little book is a narrative summary of my findings garnered from an extensive review of America's past as revealed in historical and literary documents. Weary of the incessant 24/7 biased attacks on President Trump who, in the 2016 election, rode the campaign slogan "make America great again" into the Whitehouse, I decided to go to original sources for a more objective perspective. I was delighted with my findings, so much so I felt compelled to organize them into narrative form for sharing with anyone interested in a documented perspective on What Makes America Great. And to accommodate reader convenience, I have kept the narrative succinct—as the book's small size confirms—so that it can be read in one sitting should time demand.

BOB DOWELL

WHAT MAKES AMERICA GREAT

THE GREATNESS ISSUE

Donald Trump's riding the "make America great again" wave to the White House in the 2016 presidential election not only shocked but, in varying degrees, angered and disgruntled the liberal minded establishment, not to mention some of the conservative minded establishment as well. Pundits, politicians, and celebrities immediately began expressing their disdain for Trump and his "make America great again" campaign slogan. New York Governor Cuomo expressed deep disdain by voicing his counter statement: "America was never great!" Saying make America great again presumably means that America was once great and that it can through enlightened leadership become great again. Saying America was never great presumably means America's previous existence was mediocre at best and a miserable failure at worst. One thing for sure, the country is passionately divided over the issue:

witness the 24/7 discussion and debate on cable news and social media, often conducted in a highly partisan and inflammatory manner.

Obviously, the American greatness issue is of utmost importance, but little or no valid insight comes from listening to the incessant name-calling and partisan bias. So what does one do? Having given the matter considerable thought while reviewing a mountain of American history and literature, this concerned American has put together a narrative that addresses the issue from a historical perspective, a narrative that I would very much like to share with anyone willing to listen. If you're on board, please hear me out.

Hold it: one more thing before we embark. In the interest of full disclosure, I should reveal that I grew up thinking America great. I enthusiastically repeated the Pledge of Allegiance in school and elsewhere, gave thanks for the privilege to freely worship God, and to pursue a vocation of my choice. Was I naïve? That's the question that motivated me to research and review the history and literature of our country from its beginnings, and particularly its beginnings where directives were established and foundations were laid. Now, having addressed transparency, let us embark on our investigative journey beginning with America's birth.

WHAT THE RECORD REVEALS

REFORMATION BIRTHED AND BIBLE ORIENTED

The Reformation birthed America! Sound strange? Not so strange if you know the history of the Reformation, the great religious revolution that swept Europe beginning in 1517 when Martin Luther nailed his 95 Theses on the church door in Wittenberg, Germany. This German monk and Professor of Theology sparked the Reformation by publically challenging Church practices, particularly the practice of selling indulgences, and Church doctrines, particularly the doctrine of salvation. The public debate beginning in Wittenberg spread across Europe accelerated by the newly invented Gutenberg printing press (1440). The debate, turning violent, triggered the Thirty Years' War that divided states over Catholic doctrine versus Protestant doctrine. Though the Thirty Years' War ended in 1648, the war of words continued as Protestant theologians continued their protest against Catholic doctrines by submitting their own. Subsequent to Martin Luther, John Calvin (1509-1564) emerged early on as one of the leading Protestant theologians, and particularly the one who most directly affected American thought via England. Out of his theology emerged the Puritans who, beginning near the end of the 16th century, became a strong force in England. Their goal was to "purify" the Church of England, meaning to rid it of Catholic "practices." Facing stiff resistance, a number of Puritans began looking toward the New World as a better place to pursue their mission. One early Puritan leader holding this view was John Winthrop (1587-1649), lawyer, lay minister, and founder of the Massachusetts Bay Colony (1630).

Preceding the Massachusetts Bay Colony was the school-book famous Plymouth Colony, the Mayflower Pilgrims who landed in America in 1620, led by the steadfast Puritan, William Bradford (1590-1657), the colony's long time governor. Not only did John Winthrop and William Bradford serve as long time governors of their respective colonies [then referred to as plantations], but also penned famous documents recording their burning desires and efforts to establish a God-centered commonwealth in the New World: Bradford's history, *Of Plymouth Plantation,* and

Winthrop's sermon, "A Model of Christian Charity." It is from Winthrop's sermon that we get the enduring and often quoted phrase— "city upon a hill"— when lauding America as exemplary. Winthrop debuted the phrase in defining his vision of the exemplary commonwealth that he and Bradford and these early American Puritan colonists were willing to risk their lives and fortunes to establish. No time in history has so well educated and wealthy group of people as the Massachusetts Bay Colony left their body politic to face the hazards of establishing a new one, and certainly not by further risking their lives and fortunes in crossing a perilous ocean to establish it in a wilderness. Without doubt, the primary stimulus that drove the Bay Colony to do so was their intense religious fervor. The Plymouth Colony lacked the wealth and education level of the Bay Colony, but they certainly shared their religious fervor as is well documented in Bradford's *Of Plymouth Plantation*.

His history of the colony is filled with references to providence. He interpreted events, whether good or bad, in terms of God's will. When the colonists encountered a challenging event his solace would be a providence reminder. Witness the steadfast faith revealed in his response to the colony's challenge of crossing a perilous ocean to inhibit a New World wilderness: "since their desires were set on the ways of God they must rest on His providence." Likewise, when the colony experienced a favorable event he is also quick to designate it providential. Witness the Squanto event: Squanto, a friendly Indian, who speaks English, comes to live with the struggling colony serving not only as their interpreter but also their hunting, fishing, and farming guide. Bradford describes him as "a special instrument sent of God for their good beyond their expectation." The frequent use of such phrases as "here is to be noted a special providence of God" throughout *Of Plymouth Plantation* to introduce a special event explicitly emphasizes its providence theme.

This providential view was rooted in the mindset of many early American Puritans who viewed themselves as the new Israelites called to model God's will for the world to witness. Immersed in covenant theology, they reasoned thusly: when the Israelites, God's chosen people, failed to live up to their covenant with Him, He sent his Son to establish a new covenant, this time twelve apostles instead of twelve tribes, the Church instead of the Temple. But in their view, the Church, after some fifteen hundred years, was miserably failing to carry out the new covenant; consequently, the Church must be reformed, its present practices must be purified. Yet, in their minds, a century of debate and a thirty years' war had made little progress in the needed reform. More specifically, England's break with Rome by Parliament declaring their king "the supreme head on earth of the Church of England," (the Act of Supremacy, 1534), did not bring about the reform the Puritans deemed necessary. Consequently, they reasoned it their mission to "purify" the Church and dedicated themselves to that purpose, many believing they were in a covenant relationship with God for doing so. Needless to say, their efforts often triggered persecution.

England's King James, (1603-1625), threatened "to harry them out of the land, or even worse." Consequently, the Plymouth group soon left England to live in the Netherlands for several years before coming to America, an act they viewed as providential. They belonged to the more radical Puritan reformers who were referred to as Separatists because they advocated separating from the Church of England and setting up churches outside the established order. Although the Bay Colony Puritans were not classified as Separatists, they ultimately decided that it best, even providential, they pursue their purification efforts in the wilderness of the New World where they would not be harried by the king and church officials. So in 1630, they set sail for America, arriving only a decade after the Plymouth colony.

DEDICATED TO THE EXEMPLARY AND COVENANT BOUND

On the way to the New World to set up a Bible-centered commonwealth, their leader, John Winthrop aboard the lead ship *Arbella,* penned and delivered his famous sermon, "A Model of Chriatian Charity," in which he spelled out their mission and the covenant premise on which it depended. His sermon explicitly expresses a view that became widespread among the Puritan colonists: the view of their New World mission being a covenanted mission. "Bible" and "covenant" are the catchwords in Winthrop's "A Model of Christian Charity." After explaining that by providence humanity is diverse—rich and poor, weak and strong—but ideally are bonded through Christian love, the bond of perfection, the bond to be cultivated and perpetuated by the Bay Colony. He further explains that this bond must be grounded in a covenant relationship between the colonists and God and that its success depends upon the colonists' obedience to the covenant. He writes, "Thus stands the cause between God and us. We are entered into a covenant with Him for this work. We have taken out a commission, and the Lord has given us leave to draw our own articles . . . . Now, if the Lord shall please to hear us, and bring us in peace to the place we desire, then He has ratified this covenant and sealed our commission . . . but if we shall neglect the observation of these articles which are the ends we have propounded . . . the Lord will surely break out in wrath against us; revenged of such a perjured people." For maintaining obedience to their covenant, he exhorts the colonists to follow the counsel of the Old Testament prophet Micah, "to do justly, to love mercy, to walk humbly with our God."

Doing so, Winthrop argues, will make us such "a praise and glory" that persons will say of subsequent colonies, "Lord make it like that of New England [the Bay Colony]. For we must consider that we shall be as *a city upon a hill*," a phrase echoing a passage from Jesus' Sermon on the Mount [Matthew: 5-7] in which he addresses his disciples saying, "You are the light of the world. A city that is set on a hill cannot be hidden." Unquestionably, this exemplary city upon a hill concept permeates early American literature. We see it in document after document from Winthrop's *A Model of Christian Charity* (1630) to Thomas Jefferson's Declaration of Independence (1776), a political tract promoting the exemplary. Witness the often quoted portion of the Declaration declaring under the laws of nature and nature's God, "that all men are created equal; that they are endowed by their Creator with certain inalienable rights; that among these are life liberty and pursuit of happiness." In early American literature, whether sermon, history, diary, poetry, or political tract, we see God, providence, and the exemplary motif voiced, sometimes explicitly, sometimes implicitly, but consistently expressed in document after document.

Let us note a few lines from a less well-known document, Edward Johnson's epic *Wonder-Working Providence of Sion's Savior in New England* (1654). Johnson envisioned the Puritan colonists coming to America as participants in a cosmic epic, the war between good and evil, between Christ and Satan. Thus, through an epic framework Johnson elevates the event to universal significance: the fate of humanity dependent on the success of the Puritan mission. At this point in the tumultuous cosmic war, Christ recruits an army of true believers from England for purposes of establishing an exemplary God-centered commonwealth in the New World. He writes, "When England began to decline in religion . . . Christ, the glorious king of His churches, raises an army out of our English nation, for freeing His people from their long servitude under usurping prelacy [corrupt clergy]." Johnson then envisions Christ Jesus "stirring up His servants for service in the western world and more especially for planting the united colonies of New England where you are to attend the service of the king of kings . . . to know this is the place where the Lord will create . . . new churches and a new commonwealth together." So on the voyage when "exposed to danger of tempestuous seas, show whose servants you are by calling on the name of God . . . and publishing your Master's will and pleasure to all that voyage with you that it is His mind to have purity in religion." And upon your landing, "see you observe the rule of His word, for neither larger nor stricter commission can He give any." Make sure that you "search out the mind of God both in planting and continuing church and civil government." And "let the matter and form of your churches be such as were in primitive times [New Testament church] before Antichrist's kingdom prevailed. Do all of these things and thereby "prosecute *this design* to the full."

And in Johnson's epic we pick up a new phrase for the exemplary—"this design"— to add to "the city upon a hill" phrase in describing the perceived American destiny. Thus far, we have witnessed the recurring theme—a God-centered commonwealth being established in America—repeated in three different literary genres: Winthrop's sermon, Bradford's historical narrative, and Johnson's epic. All three expound the destiny of America through a combination of imagination and reality. Winthrop's sermon recounts more what is projected to happen and the covenant conditions for it to happen; Bradford's history recounts what was happening and analyzes the events in terms of God's providence; and Johnson's epic recounts events in a graphic cosmic vision in which abstract providence becomes the embodied Christ recruiting his England servants for service in new-world America. Through his semi-fictional epic framework, Johnson imaginatively captures the zeal demonstrated by England Puritans carrying out their perceived duty to establish a purified new commonwealth in new-world America. By "this design" America is to be "a city upon a hill," an exemplary God-centered commonwealth for the world to see and to emulate.

Contributing to this design is the Mayflower Compact that Bradford records and discusses in his history. Actually, he called it " a combination made by them before they came ashore," they and them referring to the pilgrims and "strangers" arriving on the *Mayflower*, pilgrims being the Puritans, strangers being non-Puritans who sailed with them. Only later, after wide acceptance of the social compact theory of government in the works of Locke and Rousseau, was the document referred to as a compact. In Bradford's analysis of the event, we learn why the compact was drawn up. The Pilgrims had obtained a generous patent from the Virginia Company of London allowing them to establish a plantation [a colony] anywhere in the Virginia Company's vast domain and to practice self-government there, but having landed in New England placed them outside the jurisdiction of the Virginia Company domain thereby jeopardizing their patent. Their supposed invalid patent gave rise to mutinous talk among the strangers who were saying, "that coming ashore they would use their own liberty, for [under the circumstances] none had the power to command them." Such circumstances gave birth to the Mayflower Compact.

To avoid the premature termination of their dream of establishing a God-centered commonwealth in the new world, the Pilgrims, undoubtedly after much thoughtful prayer, took action to salvage their dream. They conceived and inscribed in document form what came to be known as the Mayflower Compact in the hope that its implementation would allow them to fulfill their dream. As revealed in the following quote from the document, the Pilgrims drew heavily on their Puritan background especially their covenant theology: "Having undertaken, for the Glory of God and the advancement of the Christian Faith, . . . a voyage to plant the First Colony in the Northern Parts of Virginia, do by these presents [persons present] solemnly and mutually in the presence of God and one of another, Covenant and Combine ourselves together into a Civil Body Politic, for our better ordering and preservation and furtherance of the ends aforesaid; and by virtue hereof to enact, constitute and frame such just and equal Laws, Ordinances, Acts, Constitutions and Offices, from time to time, as shall be thought meet and convenient for the general good of the Colony, unto which we promise all due submission and obedience." The document was witnessed and signed by the Pilgrims, first by John Carver, who was elected to be their governor, and second by William Bradford who, following Carver's death, served intermittently as their governor for the next thirty years.

The Pilgrims witnessing and signing their names to the Mayflower Compact may trigger in the mind of the reader the image of a later group of signers, the American patriots signing the Declaration of Independence and in doing so pledging their lives and fortunes to implementing the exemplary document. To expand the analogy, would there not be a significant measure of truth in declaring that imbedded in the Mayflower Compact are kernels of both our Declaration of Independence and our Constitution? Think of the self-evident God given "inalienable rights" premise in the Declaration and the "we the people" implied covenant bond in the Preamble of the Constitution? Or more generally, we might say that the Pilgrims' Mayflower Compact not only addressed their problem at hand, but provided, by example, future counsel as well. It is the first example in American history of the establishment of a government through mutual agreement of the people governed. Notable also, as implied in the invocation of the document, is their belief that God is the author and proprietor of all government, that the Bible is the primary resource for civil government, and that civil government functions in the framework of a covenant bond between God and the body politic. Surely we would not be remiss in saying the Mayflower Compact not only served to perpetuate the Pilgrims' exemplary dream but also continued to serve, by example, in perpetuating the exemplary motif in the ongoing American dream. Witness not only the Declaration of Independence and the Constitution, but also later documents, such as Lincoln's "Gettysburg Address" and King's "I Have a Dream," which have given famous expressions of the exemplary motif so prevalent in the America experience.

OVERCOMING SERIOUS CHALLENGES TO THE EXEMPLARY

All the groups and individuals discussed above had a dream. The Plymouth Pilgrims had a dream: to establish a God-centered commonwealth in America. The Massachusetts Bay Colonists had a dream: to establish a God-centered commonwealth in America. The Colonial Patriots had a dream: to break oppressive ties with England, as permissible under the Laws of Nature and Nature's God. The Founding Fathers had a dream: to design a government deriving its just powers from consent of the people and a written authoritative guide for its function, in short, "a more perfect union." Though ideal and exemplary, the difficulty of its embodiment has at times made the dream seem the impossible dream. But fortunately at those crucial times, remarkably exemplary persons have stepped forward to save the dream, to keep it alive for fuller embodiment. Prime example: Lincoln steps forward to save the union, a union not yet perfect, a union engaged in a civil war, a war over civil rights (the institution of slavery), a war over states rights (states rights versus federal rights). At a cementary dedication in November 1863, the third year of the war, Lincoln delivers his famous Gettysburg Address in which he places the bloody Gettysburg battle and the war as a whole in the historical context of the American dream. "Four score and seven years ago" (1863-1776) dates the birth of the nation, an embodied dream now in its 87th year but courting dismemberment.

Knowing his history and his people, and bolstered by his faith in God and the exemplary American dream, Lincoln steps forward and delivers the inspiring speech while standing on a renowned Civil War battlefield, the heavy-casualty battlefield at Gettysburg, a battle where the Union forces won a decisive battle generally thought to be the turning point of the war. In the speech he honors the men who gave their lives in the service of liberty, the men who shed their blood that all men might share the declared American dream of life, liberty, and pursuit of happiness, that the blood they shed here might inspire and consecrate a new devotion to "a government of the people, by the people, for the people," phrases echoing the expressed covenant intent "to form a more perfect union" stated in the Preamble of the Constitution.

Granted, a dream is only a dream until embodied by reality, but does not our history reveal the American dream of life, liberty, and pursuit of happiness being embodied step by step despite resistance and conflict, at times severe, the Civil War being a prime example, yet always there has been those willing to risk their lives and fortunes to promote the embodiment of the dream? Does not its embodiment begin with the landing of the Plymouth and Massachusetts Bay colonists in the 17th century? And does not its embodiment progress with the signing of the Declaration of Independence, the winning of the Revolutionary War and the framing of the Constitution, all in the 18th century? And does not its progression continue with the soul searching that climaxes in the bloody Civil War of the 19th century that initiated the passage of corrective Constitutional Amendments, and on into the 20th century with the Civil Rights Movement initiating legislation against still existing inequalities—particularly legislation against African-American inequality.

Without question, an exceptionally notable voice promoting the Civil Rights Movement of the 20th century was that of Martin Luther King, who like Abraham Lincoln a century before, stepped forward to address the nation. In delivering his famous "I Have a Dream" speech, he profoundly inspired the nation to re-examine its prolonged prejudicial attitude toward African Americans and thereby to initiate legislation enforcing their God given rights—"all men are created equal"— promised them in the Declaration of Independence and guaranteed them in the 13th, 14th, and 15th Amendments of the Constitution: the 13th freed them by abolishing slavery; the 14th gave them citizenship; and the 15th gave them the right to vote.

Standing in front of the Lincoln Memorial in August, 1963, one-hundred years after Lincoln signed the Emancipation Proclamation (January, 1863) and delivered his Gettysburg Address (also, 1863), King, a student of history, a minister of the Lord, and a master of rhetoric, holds up a moral word mirror before the nation reflecting powerful images for bending prejudicial minds and softening stony hearts. In the tradition of the founders of America, this later day prophet, preacher, rhetorician seeks to expedite the full embodiment of the American dream, the exemplary "city upon a hill." Like Winthrop and Bradford and Johnson and Jefferson and Lincoln before him, King believes in the American dream, endorses a city upon a hill image, the exemplary design, passionately believes it can be fully embodied, but sadly laments the fact that its embodiment had continued to be denied the African-American despite the Declaration's promise, the bloody Civil War's sacrifice for Constitutional Amendments specifically guaranteeing it. Compelled by the urgency of now, an impassioned Martin Luther King addresses the nation, beginning with these words, "Five score years ago, a great American, in whose shadow we stand today signed the Emancipation Proclamation."

In this first line, King unmistakably connects with Lincoln rhetorically ("five score years ago"), historically (1863/1963), and morally (the Emancipation Proclamation). The context established, King moves on to dramatize the inequality between the country's African-American citizens and its other citizens, between the promise of the American dream for African-Americans and its lack of embodiment for them. Though the Emancipation Proclamation became "a beacon light of hope to millions of Negro slaves who had been seared in the flames of withering injustice . . . one hundred years later the Negro still is not free," continues King. "One hundred years later the life of the Negro is still sadly crippled by the manacles of segregation and the chains of discrimination . . . one hundred years later, the Negro is still languished in the corners of American society and finds himself exiled in his own land." Utilizing symbolism of place, strategic repetitive phrase, and vivid descriptive imagery, King delivers a riveting mirror speech appealing to the nation to take redemptive action, to take exemplary action, to take "a city upon a hill" action.

Let's sample the compelling rhetoric and irrefutable logic of this speech that captivated and spurred a nation to action. "So we've come here today to dramatize a shameful condition. In a sense we've come to our nation's capital to cash a check." Of course, he is speaking figuratively to dramatize a point: he is using the promissory notes/bad checks/ insufficient funds extended metaphor to vividly characterize the prolonged injustice against African Americans. Figuratively speaking, they had been holding promissory notes for much longer than the one-hundred years since the Emancipation Proclamation. Figuratively speaking, they had been holding promissory notes since the Declaration of Independence's declaring "that all men are created equal; that they are endowed by their Creator with certain inalienable rights; that among these are life, liberty, and the pursuit of happiness." Figuratively speaking, when the republic's architects signed the Declaration of Independence and the Constitution "they were signing a promissory note to which every American was to fall heir. . . [yet] it is obvious today [1963] that America has defaulted on this promissory note insofar as her citizens of color are concerned." As is obvious today, King laments, "America has given the Negro people a bad check, a check that has come back marked insufficient funds." But as he goes on to say, figuratively and powerfully, it is not insufficient funds, but insufficient justice—the manacles of segregation and the chains of discrimination—that negates the promissory note for the Negro, a condition the Negro will no longer tolerate. America must realize "the fierce urgency of *now,*" for "it would be fatal for the nation to overlook the urgency of the moment and to underestimate the determination of the Negro." And enlarging the dimensions and the glare of this rhetorical moral mirror, he reflects: "*Now* is the time to rise from the dark and desolate valley of segregation to the sunlit path of racial justice. *Now* is the time to open the doors of opportunity to all of God's children." In the tradition of Winthrop's "Model of Christian Charity," King recognizes the importance of God at the center of the commonwealth for the embodiment of the city upon a hill dream.

He explains that it is not physical force, but spiritual force that forges the exemplary, a moral force emanating from the hearts of the people. He makes it abundantly clear that it is a heart changing moral force that "will lift the nation from the quick sands of racial injustice" and thereby firmly cautions his fellow African-Americans: "In the process of gaining our rightful place we must not be guilty of wrongful deeds." And therein lies King's greatness, his model of Christian charity stance and his rhetorical ability to persuade the majority of all Americans through this non-violent approach. Again, addressing his fellow African-Americans, he cautions, "Let us not seek to satisfy our thirst for freedom by drinking from the cup of bitterness and hatred . . . we must not allow our creative protest to degenerate into physical violence. Again and again we must rise to the majestic heights of meeting physical force with soul force." Particularly referencing the thousands of listeners standing before him, he continues: "The marvelous new militancy which has engulfed the Negro community must not lead us to a distrust of all white people, for many of our white brothers, as evidenced by their presence here today, have come to realize that their destiny is tied up with our destiny and their freedom is inextricably bound to our freedom."

Again, emphasizing the urgency of now, he addresses those who are asking civil rights devotees, when will they be satisfied. As if looking above to the source of the aforementioned soul power, he echoes the Bible's social justice prophet Amos saying, "we will not be satisfied until justice rolls down like waters and righteousness like a mighty stream."

Next, through brilliant rhetoric, particularly repetitive phrasing and allusion, King indelibly inscribes his dream in the mind and heart of the nation. Each repetitive "I have a dream" adds persuasive dimension. Witness the following. "I say to you today, my friends, that in spite of the difficulties and frustrations of the moment I still have a dream. It is a dream deeply rooted in the American dream. I have a dream that one day this nation will rise up and live out the true meaning of its creed: 'we hold these truths to be self-evident; that all men are created equal' . . . . I have a dream that my four little children will one day live in a nation where they will not be judged by the color of their skin but by the content of their character." And ending the repetitive "I have a dream" King uses words the prophet Isaiah used in offering hope and comfort to his fellow Jews dreaming of being freed from Babylonian captivity: "one day every valley shall be exalted, every hill and mountain shall be made low, the rough places will be made plain, and the crooked places will be made straight, and the glory of the Lord shall be revealed, and all flesh shall see it together."

The faith expressed by King, the contemporary prophet, comes from the same source as that of Isaiah, the prophet of old. The source is, of course, God, and the faith is that of Abraham, the steadfast faith which elicited from God the enduring covenant promise that through this faith all families of the earth would be blessed [Genesis 12:1-3]. Thus, after having first expressed this faith through the words of Isaiah, King adds, "With this faith we will be able to hew out of the mountain of despair a stone of hope. With this faith we will be able to transform the jangling discords of our nation into a beautiful symphony of brotherhood . . . This will be the day when all of God's children will be able to sing with new meaning, 'My country, 'tis of thee,/ Sweet land of liberty, /Of thee I sing.'" And he might have added, this will be the day when America shines forth as that "city upon a hill," that Model of Christian Charity of which colonial prophet John Winthrop dreamed and voiced at the country's beginning.

So, what is great about King's speech? First, he brilliantly places his dream convincingly within the historical context of the America dream. How could one deny his dream without denying the American dream? Second, one can, I believe, validly argue that the speech implicitly conjures not only the noble ideal meaning the exemplary implicit in American history and literature, but also the noble ideal meaning the exemplary implicit in Western Civilization: a Bible oriented world nurturing individual worth, charity and humility, law and order.

AMERICA IN CONTEXT: THE NOBLE IDEAL OF WESTERN CIVILIZATION

At this point, I suggest the reader take a few minutes and peruse the chart on page 35 that provides a graphic design of what I am calling the Noble Ideal implicit in Western Civilization. First, note the Old World time frame: Jerusalem, representing the center of Jewish culture; Athens, representing the center of Greek culture; and Rome, representing the center of Roman culture, the three cultures that shaped Western Civilization. Second, note these three cultures merging at the Cross. Third, note the New World time frame: Philadelphia, representing the center of American culture. Fourth, carefully note the quote under each cultural center: under Jerusalem, the quote from the Bible; under Athens, the quote from the *Iliad*; under Rome, the quote from the *Aeneid*; and under Philadelphia, the quote from the Declaration of Independence, each quote of the

Old World centers reflecting the respective culture's ideal, then the three merged and enhanced at the Cross by the Cross and dispersed throughout the Old World.

The maturing Noble Ideal of the Old World then takes root in New World America, its promise being voiced in the Declaration of Independence at America's early cultural center Philadelphia. Then think of America's history as the continuing maturation of the Noble Ideal promised in what has been called America's creed: "We hold these truths to be self-evident; that all men are created equal; that they are endowed by their Creator with certain inalienable rights; that among these are life, liberty, and the pursuit of happiness."

THE NOBLE IDEAL IMPLICIT IN WESTERN CIVILIZATION

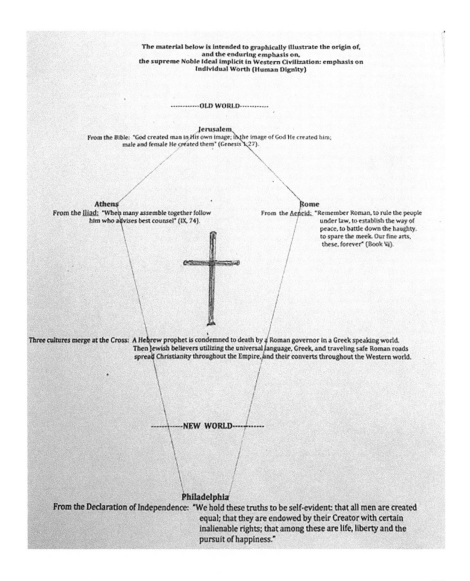

The material below is intended to graphically illustrate the origin of, and the enduring emphasis on, the supreme Noble Ideal implicit in Western Civilization: emphasis on Individual Worth (Human Dignity)

------------OLD WORLD------------

Jerusalem
From the Bible: "God created man in His own image; in the image of God He created him; male and female He created them" (Genesis 1.27).

Athens
From the Iliad: "When many assemble together follow him who advises best counsel" (IX, 74).

Rome
From the Aeneid: "Remember Roman, to rule the people under law, to establish the way of peace, to battle down the haughty, to spare the meek. Our fine arts, these, forever" (Book VI).

Three cultures merge at the Cross: A Hebrew prophet is condemned to death by a Roman governor in a Greek speaking world. Then Jewish believers utilizing the universal language, Greek, and traveling safe Roman roads spread Christianity throughout the Empire, and their converts throughout the Western world.

------------NEW WORLD------------

Philadelphia
From the Declaration of Independence: "We hold these truths to be self-evident: that all men are created equal; that they are endowed by their Creator with certain inalienable rights; that among these are life, liberty and the pursuit of happiness."

Hopefully, the succinct overview of Western Civilization depicted on the chart captures not only what I believe to be the exemplary essence (the Noble Ideal) implicit in Western Civilization, but also my belief that its fruition is the story of our American culture. The remaining narrative will address that belief.

CONTINUED EMBODIMENT OF AMERICA'S EXEMPLARY CREED: EQUALITY OF WOMEN

So, let's continue the narrative by noting the quote from the Declaration of Independence listed under Philadelphia on the chart and recall what King said, in his speech, about the words in this quote, "I have a dream that one day this nation will rise up and live out the true meaning of its creed: 'We hold these truths to be self-evident; that all men are created equal.'" He said this because he had faith in the American dream, a faith well placed.

Why do I say well placed? I say well placed because when I hear the words, or read, the words of this quote I think of America's history as the playing out of the promise inherent in its words. I see the promise of these words materializing in America's development, coming to fruition if you will. Not without debate, not without contention, and not without setbacks, nevertheless, progressing toward the ideal promised: witness the Constitution, the Bill of Rights, and later the Thirteenth Amendment (freeing the Negro), the Fourteenth Amendment, (making the Negro a citizen), the Fifteenth Amendment (giving the Negro the right to vote) the Nineteenth Amendment (giving women the right to vote), instituting the equality factor of the promise. Not only the equality of "all men," but "all persons" regardless of race, color or gender. And the phrase "all men" in the quote and the Nineteenth Amendment reference remind me that it's time in this narrative to recognize the leader who stepped forward to address women's self-evident inalienable right of equality. That leader was Elizabeth Cady Stanton, and the event is the Seneca Falls Convention (1848) that she initiated.

Who was Elizabeth Cady Stanton? She was a woman well prepared, perhaps providentially, to play her leadership role in making America great. The Cady family was a politically oriented family: her lawyer father served in Congress; her mother actively participated in his campaigns. In 1840, Elizabeth Cady married Henry B. Stanton: lawyer, journalist, social reformer, politician, and abolitionist. Both being anti-slavery activists, they traveled to London on their honeymoon in order to attend a World Anti-Slavery Convention. Much to her chagrin, all women delegates were rejected. No doubt, this slight provoked counter action in her mind, for in 1848, she initiated the call for a women's right convention to be held in Seneca Falls, New York.

With some 300 people in attendance, Elizabeth Cady Stanton presented her "Declaration of Sentiments," a document in which she resourcefully adopts the format of the masterfully written Declaration of Independence. By lifting portions verbatim, adding succinct inserts, and supplanting deletions with similar structured revisions, Stanton infuses her document with the forceful rhetorical aura of the Declaration of Independence.

The "Declaration of Sentiments" begins, "When in the course of human events it becomes necessary for one ~~people to dissolve the political bands which have connected them with another, and to assume among the powers of the earth the separate and equal station~~ [portion of the family of man to assume among the people of the earth a position different from that which they have hitherto occupied, but one] to which the laws of nature and of nature's

God entitle them, a decent respect to the opinion of mankind requires that they should declare the causes ~~which~~ [that] impel them to ~~the separation~~ such a course." Not only is the earlier document's masterful rhetoric maintained in these opening lines but its explicit providential sentiment—"the laws of nature and nature's God"—as well.

[**Note to Reader**: the lined-through words in the above paragraph are the words deleted from the Declaration of Independence in adopting its beginning as the beginning of the "Declaration of Sentiments; the words in brackets are the words supplanting the deleted words.]

Stanton continues in this manner to effectively infuse the rhetorical pattern of the masterfully worded Declaration of Independence into her document. She relegates similar injuries suffered by woman from man to those suffered by the colonists from the king of Great Britain. And she does so using the same rhetorical pattern, the use of repetition and parallel structure for strengthening the conviction brief. In the Declaration of Independence the brief is set up as follows: "The history of the present king of Great Britain is a history of injuries and usurpations, all having in direct object the establishment of an absolute tyranny over these states. To prove this let facts be submitted to a candid world." Following this general charge is a long list of specific injuries and usurpations to build a preponderance of factual evidence, and each descriptive violation beginning with the phrase "he has" to emphasize the king's repeated tyrannical acts.

The "Declaration of Sentiments" follows the same pattern: "The history of mankind is a history of repeated injuries and usurpations on the part of man toward woman, having in direct object the establishment of an absolute tyranny over her. To prove this, let facts be submitted to a candid world." Note that other than substituting "man" for "king" the "Declaration of Sentiments" follows the pattern set forth in the Declaration of Independence. It presents a long list of specific injuries and usurpations, each descriptive violation beginning with the words "he has" for purposes of keeping the focus on the violator, man, in building the preponderance of convicting evidence.

Witness several examples:

"He has never permitted her to exercise her inalienable right to the elective franchise."

"*He has* compelled her to submit to laws, in the formation of which she had no voice."

"*He has* made her, if married, in the eye of the law, civilly dead."

"*He has* taken from her all right in property, even to the wages she earns."

"*He has* denied her the facilities for obtaining a thorough education—all colleges being closed against her." [Oberlin College in 1837, first to accept women]

"*He has* usurped the prerogative of Jehovah himself, claiming it as his right to assign for her a sphere of action, when that belongs to her conscience and her God."

After finishing the "he has" preponderance of evidence, she sums up the brief saying, "Now, in view of this entire disfranchisement of one-half the people of this country, their social and religious degradation—in view of the unjust laws above mentioned, and because women do feel themselves aggrieved, oppressed, and fraudulently deprived of their most sacred rights, we insist that they have an immediate admission to all the rights and privileges which belong to them as citizens of these United States." Next, she addresses the herculean task ahead, getting these inalienable rights of women socially and legally instituted, such tasks as "petitioning state and national legislatures," enlisting "the pulpit and the press." In closing, as in the Declaration of Independence, she calls for signature pledge. "Firmly relying upon the final triumph of Right and the True, we do this day affix our signatures to this declaration." Sixty-eight women and thirty-two men signed the document.

Although Stanton, in her closing lines of "Sentiments," leaves out the "divine providence" reference included in the closing lines of the Declaration of Independence, it is given top priority in the document's attached "Resolutions," which begin as follows. "Whereas, the great precept of nature is conceded to be, 'that man shall pursue his own true and substantial happiness,' Blackstone,* in his Commentaries remarks, that this law of Nature being coeval with mankind, and dictated by God himself, is of course superior in obligation to any other. It is binding over all the globe, in all countries and at all times; no human laws are of any validity if contrary to this." *[Sir William Blackstone, author of the influential 18th century Commentaries on he Laws of England]

Following this introduction is a brief of resolves presented in the same rhetorical pattern as the "he has" violations: repetition and parallelism, each resolve beginning with the words, *"Resolved, That."* Included here are three of the twelve resolves.

"Resolved, That such laws as conflict, in any way, with the true and substantial happiness of woman, are contrary to the great precept of nature, and of no validity; for this is 'superior in obligation to any other.'"

"Resolved, That all laws which prevent woman from occupying such a station in society as her conscience shall dictate, or which place her in a position inferior to that of man, are contrary to the great precept of nature, and therefore of no force or authority."

"Resolved, That woman is man's equal—was intended to be so by the Creator, and the highest good of the race demands that she should be recognized as such."

Connecting the "Declaration of Sentiments" to the Declaration of Independence places the document solidly and memorably in the tradition of the exemplary American dream. Utilizing the highly persuasive rhetorical pattern of the Declaration of

Independence and its logical appeal to the highest authority, nature and nature's God, that is to say the Creator, Stanton's "Declaration of Sentiments" makes a compelling case for the necessity of revising the self-evident concept, "that all men are created equal." She argues that to be stated truly, two essential words must be added. Fully stated and truly confirming, the concept would read, "We hold these truths to be self-evident: that all men *and women* are created equal; that they are endowed by their Creator with certain inalienable rights; that among these are life, liberty, and the pursuit of happiness; that to secure these rights governments are instituted, deriving their powers from the consent of the governed." And, of course, the compelling case included voting rights for women, a right finally secured in 1920 when the Nineteenth Amendment was added to the Constitution.

TIME, EFFORT, PATIENCE, AND FAITH

Fruition of the noble ideal takes time and effort and patience and faith in God, the Creator. And that is what I see reflected in the history and literature of America, great effort and patience and faith in God exhibited by its people, generation after generation, in their ongoing pursuit of the noble ideal. The great leaders who step forward at crucial times in our history to push the agenda forward by creatively addressing the general public understand the magnitude of the challenge they face, yet their resolve is steadfast. Witness the pledge placed before the signers of the Declaration of Independence. "And for the support of this declaration, with a firm reliance on the protection of divine providence we mutually pledge to each other our lives, our fortunes, and our sacred honor."

History records the sacrifice that lay ahead. Families were divided, homes and properties destroyed, lives and fortunes lost, but ultimately liberty prevailed so that a Constitution could be written and ratified establishing a government of the people, by the people, and for the people as another noble patriot, four-score and seven years later had to remind the nation then engaged in a civil war to determine if that nation or any such nation so conceived and so constituted could long endure. It could and it did. Under divinely inspired leadership, it not only endured but prevailed. Reunited, the North and the South moved forward, a purged nation exemplified in the passage of Constitutional Amendments freeing its Negro slaves, making them citizens, and giving them the right to vote.

Given the nineteenth-century mindset, passage of these enhancing amendments was a remarkable achievement and an important step forward, but the noble ideal goalpost was still yards away. Challenges lay ahead as the twentieth century approached and lingered, the challenges sometimes contentious, sometimes even violent, but always met and usually with the dignity afforded by free speech and free press to promote meaningful public debate, the peaceful avenue for progress—"where many assemble together, follow him[the person] who gives best counsel"—because we are a nation dedicated to the proposition that all people are created equal with certain inalienable rights protected under a government empowered by consent of the people, so promised by our Declaration of Independence and so secured by our Constitution, and so approved and monitored by the Eye of Providence as symbolized on the Great Seal of the United States of America.

[See pages 82-83 for review of the Great Seal]

TAKING STOCK:
OTHER THREADS OF GREATNESS

Before moving forward chronologically, let's take stock of our narrative up to this point and determine what may need to be further addressed as well as what may need to be added.

For instance, some readers may be wondering why we have not addressed the Jamestown Colony (1607) that preceded both the Plymouth Colony (1620) and the Massachusetts Bay Colony (1630). The Plymouth colonists and Bay colonists came primarily looking for a place to enhance their souls. The first Jamestown colonists came primarily looking for a place to enhance their pocketbooks. That is to say that the Plymouth and Bay colonists were driven by religious motives; the Jamestown colonists were driven by profit motives. The original Jamestown colonists, 104 men and boys, backed by the Virginia Company, landed in America in May, 1607, with instructions to establish a settlement, to find gold, and to seek a water route to the Pacific (a water route to the Pacific would provide a shorter and more profitable trade route to Asia). No gold was found, nor was a shorter water route to the Pacific, but after a horrible starving time the colony did survive. The infusion of new settlers and the exercise of individual initiative and ingenuity by colonists like John Smith and John Wolfe saved the colony.

The exercise of individual initiative and ingenuity has most certainly contributed to America's greatness. The vast wilderness of seventeenth century America, a 2,500 mile wide expanse from the Atlantic east coast to the Pacific west coast filled with an abundance of natural resources, furnished momentous opportunity for those with initiative, ingenuity, and energy. Let's take Jamestown's Captain John Smith as Exhibit A. Very likely, without his leadership the colony would have failed early on.

The colony's swampy region with its brackish drinking water spawned multiple illnesses. This negative coupled with the early colonists preoccupation searching for gold, while neglecting preparation for an adequate food supply through farming and through trade with the native Indians led to devastating results. More than half of the original 104 colonists died the first year. Soon, however, things improved significantly under the leadership of the resourceful Captain John Smith. Though a young man, Smith was an experienced adventurer having left his farm home at age sixteen to spend a decade as a seaman, a mercenary soldier, a prisoner sold into slavery from which he escaped to return to England for more adventure. He signs on with the Virginia Company of London to serve a leadership position in the Jamestown colony and in doing so probably saved the colony from extinction.

Realizing the necessity of total effort on the part of every person, including the gentlemen colonists who disdained hands-on labor, Smith declared, "He who will not work shall not eat." Focusing the colony on food and shelter activity for survival and establishing trade with the local Indians, Smith greatly improved its condition. Unfortunately, he was wounded by a gunpowder explosion and returned to England.

After recovering from his gunpowder wound the indomitable Smith was determined to return to America. Though the Virginia Company denied his request to return to Jamestown, the ingenious Smith was able in 1614 to instigate an exploratory expedition in which he mapped and named the east coast from Penobscot Bay to Cape Cod for purposes of establishing settlements there. He named the newly explored and mapped area New England and began promoting settlement through his hyperbolic descriptions of the area. Interestingly, the Pilgrims seriously considered Smith for their military leader but, for whatever reasons, ended up selecting Myles Standish. They did, however, utilize Smith's maps and descriptions of New England. Though Smith lacked the Puritan religious fervor of the leaders of the Plymouth colony, he and Governor William Bradford would have agreed on one major issue: the importance of individual initiative, and the necessity of finding ways to promote it.

When the Plymouth colony, operating on a communal system to produce food, began to falter because more and more individuals declared themselves too ill or too weak to work, Governor Bradford surmised motivation to be the problem. He solved the problem by allotting each family a private plot to manage. Lo and behold! Persons who had previously been too ill or too weak to work the communal property were suddenly well enough and strong enough to work the private plots. Even the women and children were eager to work the private plots. In a short time, food production greatly increased.

Initiative and ingenuity are important characteristics for thriving anywhere, but are essential for thriving in a wilderness as Smith so aptly demonstrates in rescuing the Jamestown colony. And the kind of initiative and ingenuity demonstrated by Smith became the staple of the American settlers coping with the wilderness of the New World. Leaving the Old World and crossing the Atlantic Ocean to land on the east coast of the New World America, colonists faced a wilderness stretching thousands of miles west, north, and south teeming with natural resources, there for the taming and the taking, but only for those hearty souls exercising initiative and ingenuity. As more settlers came and those already here multiplied, movement continued further and further into the wilderness. America became the great frontier as settlers spread across the continent. The American frontier may be said to have lasted almost 300 years, from the 1607 Jamestown settlement to the Census Bureau announcement of the end of the frontier in 1890 when there seemed to be no discernable major tracks of land untouched by settlement. And during that time what has been called the pioneer spirit became a staple of the American psyche: heartiness, initiative, ingenuity, self-reliance. This pioneer spirit thus defined has unquestionably contributed to America's greatness. Historian Frederick Jackson Turner (1861-1932), originator of the "frontier thesis," argues that the presence of the frontier fostered an individualistic, self-reliant, democratic spirit in Americans. And I might add, a spirit that continued as America faced new frontiers other than land wilderness. American initiative and ingenuity, accommodated by democratic freedom to invent and experiment, has catapulted America to world leadership.

Sadly, however, America seems to be losing its frontier spirit as big government tends to restrict initiative and ingenuity by excessive regulation. America may be said to have begun as the great experiment, spirited colonists willing to leave the settled Old World for an unsettled New World in order to try new and modified approaches and ideas in their pursuit of a better life. The American wilderness furnished them that opportunity. Witness the Plymouth colony and the Bay colony, Puritan groups, coming with the intent of establishing an exemplary God-centered commonwealth; the Thirteen Colonies declaring their independence from England with the intent to form a more perfect union in which all men were considered to have been created equal, according to nature and the God of nature, and with certain inalienable rights among which are life liberty and pursuit of happiness. The great experiment continued to the point of a civil war testing whether America or any nation so conceived could form the more perfect union, a government of the people, by the people, for the people. A measure of confirmation was demonstrated in the adding of three amendments to the Constitution freeing the Negro slaves, making them citizens, and giving them the right to vote, then in the early twentieth century adding another Constitutional amendment giving voting rights to women, and by mid-twentieth century the country engaged in a vigorous civil rights debate resulting in legislation and court rulings assuring the reality of equal opportunity in the pursuit of happiness to all citizens regardless of gender, race, or creed.

AMERICA, THE GREAT EXPERIMENT

It may be said that America is a great experiment testing the hypothesis that a God centered commonwealth is the best possible choice. Furthermore, it may said that this great experiment began with the Plymouth and Bay Colonies presuming a covenant agreement with the omniscient, omnipresent, and omnipotent God of the Bible to establish an exemplary commonwealth in America, that commonwealth being modeled on the exemplary "city upon a hill" described in John Winthrop's "A Model of Christian Charity." Also, there are two other early documents that, in a less direct manner, may be said to reflect the God centered commonwealth hypothesis. The two documents I have in mind are Michael Wigglesworth's *The Day of Doom* and Ben Franklin's *The Way to Wealth*. So, at this point, let's return momentarily to the early era of the great experiment for purposes of reviewing these two documents which happen to be the two best selling books in early America and which exemplify, indirectly, the exemplary element of the great experiment. And in the case of *The Way to Wealth,* we will review not only the exemplary exemplified in the book, but the exemplary exemplified in the life of its author, Ben Franklin.

The Day of Doom was the number one bestseller from its publication in 1662 until overtaken by *The Way to Wealth* in 1758. Why did a long narrative poem entitled *Day of Doom* reign as best seller for almost a hundred years? It did so because of the poet author's ability to translate the colonists' abstract Calvinist theology into a personalized narrative, a narrative that transformed theological abstractions into embodied heart-felt experiences. Also, focusing on Judgment Day gave the poet greater opportunity for addressing the various categories of sin and the consequences of each category as its practitioners faced judgment. All categories were being judged and sentenced. No person was to be overlooked; no sin was to be overlooked. As the narrative declares, "It's vain, moreover for men to cover the least iniquity:/ The Judge has seen, and privy been to all their villainy./ He unto light, and open sight the works of darkness brings:/ He doth unfold both new and old, both known and hidden things." [Stanza 57] The fate of the unrighteous is sealed indiscriminately: "The glorious Judge will privilege nor emperor, nor king:/ But everyone that hath mis-done doth into judgment bring./ And every one that hath mis-done, the judge impartially/ Condemneth to eternal woe, and endless misery." [Stanza 52]

Translating cognitive abstract theology into emotive poetic narrative greatly facilitates connecting consent of heart with conviction of mind. Thus, it is not surprising this poem, at least large portions of it, were committed to memory by many New England Puritans who were taught it with their catechism. It is not surprising this poem about Judgment Day was so important to colonists believing in a God centered commonwealth. When living life under the aspect of eternity, Judgment Day is of utmost importance, for it's the day that confirms whether you spend eternity in perpetual punishment or perpetual glory. As figuratively prophesied in the Book of Matthew, "when the Son of Man shall come in his glory, then shall he sit on his throne of glory: and before him shall be gathered all the nations: and he shall separate them one from another, as the shepherd separates the sheep from the goats." In this figuratively stated prophecy, the sheep represent the righteous and the goats represent the unrighteous, "and these [the unrighteous] go away into eternal punishment; but the righteous into eternal life." [25:31-46] Reading or hearing *The Day of Doom* reminded the reader or hearer not only of the necessity of righteous living but also the importance of living in a righteous commonwealth to help facilitate righteous living. The numerous implied "do and do not do acts" vividly illustrated in the 224 stanzas of *The Day of Doom* not only create a composite ideal to follow but also dramatize the consequences of not following it. Thus, *The Day of Doom* played a significant role in perpetuating America's exemplary "city upon a hill" worldview. And the fact that after almost a century [1662—1758] *The Way to Wealth* overtook *The Day of Doom* as early America's number one bestseller does not mean that it replaced it. It did not replace; it supplemented. Let me explain, and let me do so by connecting thematically *The Day of Doom* and *The Way to Wealth* through a few poetic lines.

To Heaven, first priority, *they unanimously gave
For life, they all knew, extends beyond the grave.
Else why did our Creator us a manual give,
The Bible, to prepare us for an afterlife to live?

*[Puritans and other believers]

To foster earthly prosperity, was their second priority,
Industry and frugality they declared an absolute necessity.
Worship and work they gave the highest priority
Declaring these two virtues the most exemplary.
Wisely they extolled them, thereby the colonists stayed on track.
That they did so, I wish to substantiate through indisputable fact.

From 1662 to 1757, religious book *The Day of Doom* topped the best seller's list.
For a century, this poetical description of the Last Judgment trumped all the rest.
Then in 1758, Franklin's *The Way to Wealth* catapulted into first place.
Though it moved into first place, it did not *The Day of Doom* replace.
Side by side, the theological and the economic stood
Expounding both the spiritual and the secular virtues good.

The perceptive Franklin knew the two were inextricably intertwined.
Allow me to explicate his wise thinking by paraphrasing it in poetic line.

Do not, he cautions, depend exclusively on your own
industry and frugality
Though exemplary virtues, unquestionably, they may
at any time blasted be
Without the blessing of Heaven humbly received;
Therefore, seek that blessing: be not self-deceived.

Franklin, though not a Puritan himself, was of Puritan
parentage. In his autobiography he explains his faith
by saying, "I never doubted, for instance, the existence
of a Deity; that he made the world and governed it
by his Providence; that the most acceptable service
of God was the doing good to man; that our souls
are immortal; and that all crime will be punished,
and virtue rewarded, either here or hereafter." In
connecting virtue and wealth, he says, "nothing is
so likely to make man's fortune as virtue," a topic he
develops in a concise and creative little publication
entitled *The Way to Wealth.* This work became an
instant bestseller catapulting ahead of the century's
bestseller, *The Day of Doom.* However, it was not a
replacement; it was more like a mutually beneficial
symbiotic relationship. Both works promoted virtue:
The Day of Doom promoting virtue primarily for
purposes of assuring a glorious life hereafter; *The Way
to Wealth* promoting virtue primarily for purposes of

assuring a commendable life here but recognizing virtue as essential to both life here and hereafter and that the validity of all perceived virtue is subject to Providential approval. Recognizing the spiritual and the secular to be inextricably intertwined, Franklin cautioned do not depend exclusively on your own industry and frugality, though exemplary virtues, unquestionably, they may any time blasted be without the blessing of Heaven humbly received. Therefore, seek that blessing: be not deceived. The secular and the spiritual must be in sync, for Heaven above takes precedent over the secular below, as Franklin surmised saying any perceived virtue may blasted be without the blessing of Heaven humbly received. Thus, he reasoned, nothing is so likely to make man's fortune as virtue, so it is imperative to determine what is virtue and master it. And in his autobiography, Franklin reveals his list of thirteen perceived virtues and the plan he developed for mastering them. First though, let's review how Franklin got his start.

In a sense Franklin was a pioneer as were most early Americans, landing on its east coast hoping to bring their exemplary dreams to fruition in the New World wilderness, a process, as mentioned earlier, that continued for almost three hundred years (1607—1890). Waves of new arrivals joining numerous still restless earlier arrivals, or their descendants, continued the movement west across the vast wilderness between the east coast and the west coast. Even Franklin moved westward to Philadelphia from Boston to escape the tyranny of his printer brother to whom he was apprenticed. There, experienced and independent, he was able to find work as a printer and through the ingenious exercise of industry and frugality transform a part-time job into a highly successful printing business. Most families at the time depended on an annually published almanac for information concerning events of the forthcoming year: a calendar, weather forecasts, the rising and setting times of the sun and the moon, phases of the moon, tide tables, farm planting dates, astronomical and astrological events, and other events of interest; consequently, publishing an almanac was good business. To best the competition of other printers, the ingenious Franklin assumed the pseudonym "Poor Richard," a wise and witty character who possessed a reservoir of proverbs and sayings that he sprinkled through the almanac making it not only interesting reading but also providing practical counsel for the reader, so much so, it quickly became New England's most popular almanac, thereby earning Franklin a handsome income.

Simply establishing a handsome income, or accumulating wealth for the sake of wealth was not, however, Franklin's goal as he, through Poor Richard confirms, "tis hard for an empty bag to stand upright" meaning not having to cope with poverty frees one to pursue virtue. In Franklin's view, wealth is a virtue because, rightly used, it serves a higher purpose. This insight, along with numerous others, persona Poor Richard strategically recounts throughout *The Way To Wealth* and does so in an effective and entertaining way: story form, a genre designed to instruct and entertain as the ingenious Franklin was not only well aware, but exceeding adept in utilizing. In the work's introduction, Franklin explains that he first published his Almanac in 1732 under the name Richard Saunders [Poor Richard], that he endeavored to make it both entertaining and useful, and that it became so much in demand he vended annually near ten thousand copies which provided him considerable profit. Furthermore, noting that hardly a neighborhood in the province went without it, he saw it a proper vehicle for conveying instruction among the common people who purchased scarcely any other books (perhaps excluding *The Day of Doom*). Consequently, he began filling the small spaces between the days in the calendar with Poor Richard's proverbial sayings. For example, and as mentioned earlier, he repeats Poor Richard's proverb "it is hard for an empty sack to stand up-right" to illustrate and confirm that industry and frugality are not only means of procuring wealth but that wealth in turn is greatly helpful in securing virtue, for it is difficult for a person in want to always act honestly. Readers could not get enough of Poor Richard's proverbs.

Realizing the value of the proverbs his Poor Richard persona had sprinkled through his almanacs for more than two decades, "proverbs which contained the wisdom of many ages and nations," Franklin "assembled and formed into a connected discourse" and prefixed it to the Almanac of 1757. Its story line features Richard Saunders [Poor Richard] joining "a great number of people collected at a "vendue of merchant goods." While waiting for the sale to begin, they converse about the badness of the times. After a bit, they call upon "a plain clean old man, with white locks, 'Pray, Father Abraham, what think you about the times? Won't these heavy taxes quite ruin the country? How shall we ever be able to pay them? What would you advise us do?'"

Father Abraham stands and replies, "If you'd have my advice, I'll give it to you in short, for 'a word to the wise is enough,' and 'many words won't fill a bushel,' as Poor Richard says." Gratified upon hearing himself quoted, Saunders remains, presumably incognito, listening intently and reporting Father Abraham's address all the while supplementing it with his own supportive commentary. Utilizing this narrative framework, Franklin is able to restate and reconfirm the wisdom of numerous proverbs from the various earlier almanacs by having Father Abraham lace his enlightening address with those proverbs, each followed by the phrase, "as Poor Richard says." Utilizing this clever narrative framework, Franklin is able to entertain and instruct readers simultaneously, thus enhancing the work's appeal.

A number of the proverbs or adages popularized in this revered narrative are still current and quoted. Who has not heard "early to bed and early to rise makes one healthy, wealthy, and wise"?

Interestingly, Father Abraham reminds the gathering that though they are rightfully concerned about grievous taxes levied by the government they may not be aware "of taxes even more grievous levied by our idleness, our pride, and our folly, not one of which government commissioners can ease or deliver us. However, let us harken to good advice," he cautions, "and something may be done for us; *God helps those who helps themselves*, as Poor Richard says in his almanac of 1733." Franklin continues the narrative in this vain focusing heavily on "initiative" and "frugality," declaring the two inextricably intertwined. "*If you would be wealthy*, says he [Poor Richard] in another almanac, *think of saving as well as giving: the Indies have not made Spain rich because her outgoes are greater than her incomes?*" And thus Franklin continues the revered narrative whose purpose is not the promotion of wealth as an end in itself but as a means for enhancing a virtuous life.

This little literary masterpiece became known as *The Way to Wealth* and was so well received that its sells soon surpassed those of the century-old New England bestseller *The Day of Doom*. Though, as previously stated, *The Way of Wealth* did not replace *The Day of Doom*, it complemented: connecting the theological and the economic, the secular and the spiritual. To repeat: Franklin advocates wealth not for self-aggrandizement, but for virtue enhancement. Franklin's wealth thesis may be stated thusly: wealth makes it less difficult to live a virtuous life, and a virtuous life is the will of God, the Creator of heaven and earth.

In stating his religious creed, Franklin expresses belief in one God, Creator of the Universe, who governs by his providence, who ought to be worshipped. And that the most acceptable service we render Him is doing good to his other children. [Franklin states his religious creed in a letter to Ezra Stiles, 1790 and in his autobiography]

Franklin's life gives indisputable witness to his herculean effort to live by his religious creed. Becoming independently wealthy by age forty-two, he retired from his lucrative printing business to devote full time to serving his community and his country even though he had made major contributions before retiring having founded a public library, established a fire department, founded an academy that developed into the University of Pennsylvania, served as secretary of the American Philosophical Society, and invented an energy saving stove. It should also be

noted that Franklin refused to patent his inventions—
e. g., the Franklin stove, the lightening rod, bifocals—
declaring that "we should be glad of an opportunity
to serve others by any inventions of ours; and this we
should do freely and generously." Is this not living the
exemplary life? The exemplary was Franklin's focus.
He was determined to live life as perfectly as possible
and even developed a personal system for doing
so. First, he determined what he believed to be the
essential virtues for doing so and succinctly defined
each one. Below are his thirteen perceived virtues:

Temperance: Eat not to dullness; drink not to
elevation.

Silence: Speak not but what may benefit others or
yourself; avoid trifling conversation.

Order: Let all your things have their places; let each
part of your business have its time.

Resolution: Resolve to perform what you ought;
perform without fail what you resolve.

Frugality: Make no expense but to do good to others
or yourself; waste nothing.

Industry: Lose not time; be always employed in something useful; cut off all unnecessary actions.

Sincerity: Use no hurtful deceit; think innocently and justly, and, if you speak, speak accordingly.

Justice: Wrong none by doing injuries, or omitting the benefits that are your duty.

Moderation: Avoid extremes; forbear resenting injuries so much as you think they deserve.

Cleanliness: Tolerate no uncleanliness in body, clothes, or habitation.

Tranquility: Be not disturbed at trifles, or at accidents common or unavoidable.

Chastity: Use the sex urge but for health or offspring, never to dullness, weakness, or the injury of your own or another's peace or reputation.

Humility: Imitate Jesus and Socrates.

[Franklin lists these thirteen virtues and
their definitions in his autobiography]

After defining the thirteen virtues he considered essential for living a perfect life, he fashioned "a little book" for the purpose of monitoring his progress in exercising these virtues. The little book contained a page devoted to each virtue. At top of page was listed the virtue and its definition. At left side of page he listed, in vertical order, the initial for each virtue; at the top of the page, in horizontal order, he listed the initial for each day of the week; then he drew parallel lines across the page between each virtue and vertical lines between each day of the week, thus providing a blank square for each day of the week for each virtue. The procedure was to carefully monitor his daily performance of all thirteen virtues but, beginning with T (Temperance), to particularly concentrate on one virtue each week until all were mastered. A black mark was placed in the appropriate square for each violation of a virtue.

Franklin noted that the thirteen virtues would theoretically allow four sessions per year, there being fifty-two weeks in a year. For sure, Franklin subscribed to Socrates' famous dictum: "know thyself; the unexamined life is not worth living." Note that the succinct definition for his thirteenth virtue, H (Humility), reads: "Imitate Jesus and Socrates."

It is also important to note that Franklin connected his thirteen virtues to Heaven above. He said that conceiving God to be the fountain of wisdom he thought it necessary to seek His assistance in attaining it. For that purpose, he formed a prayer to recite daily asking for that assistance: "O powerful Goodness! Bountiful Father! Merciful Guide! increase in me that wisdom which discovers my truest interest! Strengthen my resolutions to perform what that wisdom dictates. Accept my kind offices to thy other children as the only return in my power for thy continual favors to me." This prayer he affixed to his little self-examination book.

Franklin says that the execution of his self-examination plan continued steadily for some time revealing many more faults than he had imagined, but furnishing him the satisfaction of seeing them diminish to the point he went through only one course a year and still later omitting the process entirely, but always carried "my little book" with me, presumably a constant reminder to stay on course. Very late in life, he expresses in his autobiography great satisfaction in the results of his self-examination plan saying, "it may be well my posterity should be informed that to this little artifice with the blessings of God, their ancestor owed the constant felicity of his life, down to his 79th year, in which this is written."

Retired from his printing business, Franklin not only devotes his time to serving his country, he becomes one of its most noteworthy of the founding fathers having a major role in the drafting the Declaration of Independence (1776) and The Constitution (1787), and was a signer of both documents as well, being the oldest framer at age 81, to sign the Constitution. As minister to France he was highly effective in the negotiation of the Treaty Alliance with France (1778), an alliance providing the necessary assistance for our winning of the Revolutionary War, and also the negotiation of the Treaty of Paris (1783) that ended the Revolutionary War. Franklin was also signer of these two documents making him the only founding father to sign all four of the key foundational documents establishing the United States of America: The Declaration of Independence, The Treaty of Alliance with France, The Paris Peace Treaty, and The Constitution.

The life of Ben Franklin notably reflects the exemplary principles on which America was founded: belief in God the Creator, belief in a God centered commonwealth, belief that America was to be that exemplary commonwealth, that city upon a hill. Would he not be exhibit par excellence for Winthrop's envisioned model of Christian charity, a model for all the world to see? And did he not play a major role in establishing the exemplary foundation of America, that city upon a hill.

And another exhibit par excellence for confirming that those original exemplary principles—belief in God the Creator, belief in a God centered commonwealth, belief that America was to be that exemplary commonwealth—were still very much alive and well at midpoint twentieth century as evidenced by a law passed in joint resolution by the 84th Congress in 1956 declaring the phrase "In God We Trust" to be the nation's official motto and that it must be printed on American paper currency. The phrase had been printed on American coins since the Civil War, a time when religious sentiment had been especially strong. Likewise, the impetus behind the 1956 legislation was, no doubt, the strong threat posed by communist doctrine at the time. Representative Charles Edward Bennett is said to have introduced the bill in the House saying, "in these days when imperialistic and materialistic communism seeks to attack and destroy freedom, we should continually look for ways to strengthen the foundations of our freedom."

It should also be noted that in this same time frame (1954) Congress also passed legislation officially adding the phrase "under God" into the Pledge of Allegiance. Events triggering this legislation are noteworthy as well. A sermon preached on Lincoln Day by the Reverend George M. Docherty, pastor of the New York Avenue Presbyterian Church in Washington, D. C., the church President Lincoln had regularly attended, seems to have had a strong impact on those in attendance including President Eisenhower, who sat in the Lincoln pew, as well as Congressional representatives who also attended.

Reverend Docherty stated there was something missing in the Pledge of Allegiance, "and that which was missing was the characteristic and definitive factor in the American way of life. Indeed apart from the mention of the phrase, the United States of America, it could be the pledge of any republic." One could envision hearing citizens of the Soviet Union reciting "a similar pledge to their hammer and sickle flag."

Hardly by coincidence, the very next day U S Representative Charles Oakman introduced a joint resolution to add the phrase "under God" into the Pledge of Allegiance saying, "I think Mr. Docherty hit the nail squarely on the head. One of the most fundamental differences between us and the Communists is our belief in God."

Two days later U S Senator Homer Ferguson introduced the Senate joint Resolution saying, "our nation is founded on a fundamental belief in God, and the first and most important reason for the existence of our government is to protect the God-given rights of our citizens." A few months later these joint resolutions were passed and on Flag Day, June 14, 1954, President Dwight Eisenhower signed the bill into law thereby officially adding the phrase "under God" into the Pledge of Allegiance. He praised the inclusion of the "under God" phrase saying, "from this day forward the millions of our school children will daily proclaim in city and town, every village and rural school house, the dedication of our nation and our people to the Almighty. To anyone who truly loves America, nothing could be more inspiring than to contemplate the rededication of our youth, on each school morning, to our country's true meaning."

ENTER A BLINDNESS AND DEAFNESS PHASE

Sadly, a half century or so later American society seems to care less and less about the phrase "under God" in our Pledge of Allegiance or the phrase "in God we trust" on our currency. Eyes and ears seem more and more closed to the exemplary foundational principles embedded in our historical documents. The explicit "in God we trust" phrase on our currency aside, I wonder how many people appreciate or even recognize the several implicit exemplary symbols embedded on the dollar bill, a dimension seen and handled by millions of people every day. Have you ever examined the dollar bill for that purpose? If not, I invite you to join me in doing so.

Looking at the image of the dollar bill provided on the next page, or holding a dollar bill of your own, let's note a few of the implicit exemplary images.

THE DOLLAR BILL
(OBVERSE AND REVERSE)

On the front of the dollar bill is the image of our exemplary first president, George Washington. On the back of the dollar bill is the image of the Great Seal of the United States, obverse and reverse (its front and back). On the reverse is the Eye of Providence positioned above an unfinished pyramid of thirteen layers and capped by the Latin phrase *Annuit Coeptis*. The Latin phrase is a motto explaining the symbolism of the eye image. Translated, it means "He [God] approves our undertaking," an undertaking meaning the thirteen colonies that became the first thirteen states of the United States represented by the thirteen layers of the unfinished pyramid, symbolically a new nation represented by the ancient symbol of strength and permanence, the pyramid, guided and approved by the Eye of Providence. On the bottom layer of the pyramid is its founding date inscribed in Roman numerals MDCCLXXVI—1776. Then beneath the pyramid is the Latin phrase *Novus Ordo Seclorum* meaning "A New Order Of the Ages," the New Order Of The Ages being the founding of the exemplary America.

On the obverse image of the Great Seal is the bald eagle with the shield of the United States of America. The shield has thirteen red and white stripes representing the thirteen original colonies that became the thirteen original states establishing the United States of America. To confirm, the eagle holds in its beak a banner on which is inscribed the Latin phrase *E pluribus unum,* meaning "out of many one." The eagle also holds an olive branch in the right talon, suggesting preference for peace, but a bundle of arrows in the left talon, suggesting readiness and strength for battle if necessary. Centered above the head of the eagle is a constellation of thirteen stars indicating a blessed new nation taking its place and rank among the sovereign nations of the world.

Creating the highly symbolic Great Seal was a serious matter for the founding fathers. The Continental Congress began planning a seal only hours after the signing of the Declaration of Independence in 1776. The planning, however, continued through three committees and six years of debate and revision before a final design was approved by Congress in 1782.

DISTURBING

The apparent lack of awareness, not to mention concern, of why America is great and the process by which it became great is disturbing. Seemingly, just a cursory review of that process should delight every American and motivate that person to make a special effort to continue the exemplary process begun by our founding fathers. Of course, it is important to understand our past in order to address our future. And, obviously that is what this treatise is about, reviewing our past to determine where we stand. Perhaps we can add further clarity by summarizing how well America has implemented its creed as stated in the Declaration of Independence, 1776: "We hold these truths to be self-evident that all men*[_____] are created equal, that they are endowed by their Creator with certain inalienable rights, that among these are life, liberty, and the pursuit of happiness."

*Note to Reader: *[and women]* See the Declaration of Sentiments, 1848, and the Nineteenth Amendment, 1920.

Have we not, in the ensuing years, made commendable progress in implementing the reality of our creed? Of course, we have! Witness the examples presented in this treatise. Also, keep in mind that at best societal change is generally a slow, laborious process, and perhaps rightfully so, for even change that comes after extended free and open debate may not in practice live up to theory and expectation. It may need adjustment, modification, or even nullification. Fortunately though, America has been blessed with a compass of exemplary founding principles and thereby able to keep the great experiment on course. Sadly, however, the present hateful partisan wrangling gives rise to more than a little apprehension about its future.

I'm reminded of William Butler Yeats' poem "The Second Coming" that addresses the precariousness of founding principles. Yeats employs a falcon/falconer metaphor to make his point, the falconer representing the founding principles and the falcon representing society. In the poem, a speaker contemplates the dawning of the twentieth century, speculating on what it will bring. As the title indicates, Yeats plays on the Christian belief in the second coming of Jesus Christ and uses the presumed glory of the expected occasion to dramatize what could go wrong if the founding principles lose their hold on society. The speaker envisions the falcon, in a widening gyre, moving further and further away from the falconer, so far away the falconer's commands cannot be heard. Without the falconer's commands, "the best lack all conviction, while the worst are full of passionate intensity . . . anarchy is loosed upon the world." The vision of a glorious second coming is lost. It is replaced by a jarring vision of an inglorious second coming, a "rough beast, its hour come round at last, slouches towards Bethlehem to be born." Through skillful use of narrative, allusion, and metaphor, Yeats dramatizes the importance of society not drifting out of the range of its founding principles.

It is worth noting that the case may not always be, figuratively speaking, the falcon not hearing the commands of the falconer. It can be a case of the falconer sending commands contrary to the society's founding principles. Such contrary commands also give rise to confusion and disillusionment. I call to mind the poem "Dover Beach" in which, again figuratively speaking, the falcon is hearing contrary commands from the falconer, commands contrary to the traditional ones that has shaped its worldview. The speaker in the poem dramatically narrates his confusion and disillusionment resulting from the contrary commands he is hearing. Facing a window, the speaker, gaze focused on the beach, observes a long line of spray "where the sea meets the moon-bleached land." Listening, he hears the grating roar of full-tide waves that recede and then return bringing "the eternal note of sadness in." Sadness to his ear because metaphorically the sea becomes the blanket of faith [the Judeo/Christian world view] that once embraced "the round earth's shore," but now he only hears "its vast withdrawing roar retreating . . . down the vast edges drear and naked shingles of the world."

Why the perceived gloom? The time frame is 1867, soon after Darwin's publication of *On the Origin of Species* describing evolution by natural selection, a theory widely viewed as contrary to the Genesis account of creation and thereby a denial of the Judeo/Christian world view, metaphorically the Sea of Faith whose vast withdrawing roar the "Dover Beach" speaker hears retreating "down the vast edges drear and naked shingles of the world," leaving a faithless and gloomy world.

Though these two poems were neither written by American poets nor specifically address the American experience, I feel they masterfully illustrate, figuratively, the power of a society's founding principles and the resulting devastation when their commands are no longer clearly heard. America's greatness has been its ability to not only continue to hear the commands of its founding principles but to listen judiciously in order to "form a more perfect union." Have we, on occasion, failed to listen judiciously? Of course we have! But fortunately, or perhaps providentially, wise and judicious voices nudged us back on course, prime examples being Abraham Lincoln and Martin Luther King as we have noted previously in our discussion of the "Gettysburg Address" and "I Have a Dream."

Sadly, America is presently experiencing a time of confusion, a time when its founding principles are dimly heard by many and rejected by others. We see the paralysis caused by blatant partisanship in the U. S. Congress, where political party interest too often takes precedent over the good of the country.

Will a wise and judicious voice nudge us back on course? Many think that voice may be the voice of Donald Trump whose "Make America Great Again" campaign catapulted him into the Whitehouse in 2016, yet fierce opposition rages against that voice, and it is too early to know how this controversy will play out.

The media, for the most part, rails against Trump randomly calling him a racist, a fascist, a liar, a womanizer, or whatever demeaning label comes to mind in order to declare him morally unfit to be President. Politicians and celebrities rant against him as well. For example, California Congress woman Maxine Waters has, on occasion, passionately expressed her disdain for President Trump by leading audiences in chanting "Impeach 45!" And comedian Stephen Colbert excoriates him mercilessly on his late night TV show. Conversely, Trump has his strong defenders. Notably strong is the so-called conservative Religious Right, many of whom believe Trump's election victory the will of God. Evangelist Franklin Graham is reported to have said, "I believe at this election, God showed up."

Regardless of how a person views the Religious Right, that America was founded on the concept of a God centered commonwealth is historically accurate. Secular ranting will not change that fact. Is it not despicable behavior to demonize anyone for appreciating that fact and sharing that belief? Does it not violate the Eighth Commandment—"thou shall not bear false witness"—and the Golden Rule—"do to others as you would have them do to you."? Figuratively speaking, is the falcon no longer hearing the falconer's signals? Is the Sea of Faith receding "down the vast edges drear and naked shingles of the world'? Are our Providence directed exemplary principles being eroded by self-serving, secular directed political correctness?

Where is the corrective voice that can stir the hearts and minds of America back to its exemplary founding principles? Somewhere in the great Spirit Mundi surely a contemporary Jefferson or Stanton or Lincoln or King is reaching out to reign in our widening gyre that all may hear the foundational exemplary commands at its center lest things fall apart. Let us pray for that corrective voice! And that we recognize it when it comes!

And one more thing: Could it be we're hearing it already? Could Trump be that voice crying in the wilderness preparing the way? Or—do I dare say it—could Trump be that voice? The 2020 election will surely give us a clue!

ALSO BY BOB DOWELL

Understanding the Bible: Head and Heart
Part One—The Old Testament

Understanding the Bible: Head and Heart
Part Two—Matthew through Acts

Understanding the Bible: Head and Heart
Part Three—Romans through Revelation

Papa, Tell Us About the Bible

Satan and Me and OBE:
An Out of Body Experience

These books available in paperback and e-book at
Amazon.com and **BarnesandNoble.com**
(For quick access type in author's name: Bob Dowell)

[Author Bob Dowell, PhD, brings an engaging freshness to traditional Biblical thought through creative utilization of genre: ***poetry*** in Understanding the Bible: Head and Heart; ***drama*** in Papa, Tell Us About the Bible; and ***dialogue*** in Satan and Me and OBE.]

CPSIA information can be obtained
at www.ICGtesting.com
Printed in the USA
BVHW071354130519
548119BV00007B/715/P

9 781950 540716